Sassy
the Squirrel Monkey

Anna Taylor Stevens
Illustrations by Martina Terzi

Copyright © 2021 by Anna Taylor Stevens
All rights reserved. No portion of this book may be reproduced, stored in a retrieval system, or transmitted in any form or by any means, electronic, mechanical, photocopying, recording, or otherwise, without written permission of the publisher.

Published and printed in the United States by Squirrel Monkey Publishing, LLC

ISBN: 978-0-578-97915-1

Illustrations by Martina Terzi
https://martinaterzi.carbonmade.com

Thank you, Carloyn Goyer, for your help with edits.

For more information regarding permissions, licensing, or to book an event, please email:
info@SquirrelMonkeyPublishing.com

For information on special discounts for bulk purchases, please contact:
info@SquirrelMonkeyPublishing.com

A note to young reader friends:
This is the rights page. Writing a book is the fun and easy part. Getting this book into your hands requires a tremendous amount of effort, detail, and tedious work. This is where the person/people who made this book say, "We worked hard to make this book happen because we had the discipline to deal with a bunch of legal, adult stuff which goes along with this book. We're being safe by protecting the work we put in your hands." -Anna

For everyone and especially Jack,
We come into this world full of light and love - already fully stocked with our unique gifts and interests. Tap into what marvels and excites you, embrace your infinite light and let it shine.

"All that I am, or hope to be, I owe to my mother." - Abraham Lincoln

In Loving Memory of
Sally Stevens Carlisle
(1975 ∞ 2021)

READ Guide: *Sassy the Squirrel Monkey*

READ to make a difference for a lifetime.

READ is a way to have meaningful conversations using a book to promote thinking, enhance comprehension, build vocabulary and deepen relationship with a child.

1st READ — FOCUS ON EVENTS

The first time you read, use think-alouds to teach vocabulary, introduce key events, and help the child understand the story problem and relate to the character. Use voices, expressions, tone and pace to bring the story to life.

Look at the cover, read the title and author and say "The name of this book is *Sassy the Squirrel Monkey*. Look at Sassy!" (Point to Sassy on the cover.) What kind of animal is she? ("That's right, a monkey!") She's in a tree. Wonder what will happen next? Let's read this book and find out what Sassy is doing on her journey through the jungle." As you read, explain any words your child may not understand like *compass*, *reckless* or *troop*. Act out words like *stress* and *shadow*. Point to illustrations as you say the words to help support vocabulary. After the first read, say "We just read about Sassy the Squirrel Monkey and her worries while trying to make friends. Let's look back at every one she met." (Flip back through the book and identify each new friend.)

Ask open-ended questions: "how" or "why" to encourage children to discuss key events and characters

2nd READ — CALL OUT EMOTIONS

The second time you read, use think-alouds to teach vocabulary and characters' thoughts and feelings related to key events. Remember to use expression in your voice to bring joy to reading.

Before reading, say, "Do you remember Sassy and her time in the jungle trying to make new friends? Let's read and find out how Sassy felt." Say things like, "Sassy looks anxious. She is worried about meeting new friends!" Use this read to talk about how everyone is different, and the importance of loving yourself just the way you are. "How did Sassy feel about making new friends?" "What was Sassy worried about when she realized she was different?" or "How did Sassy make her 'heart shine?'"

Point to words, act-out phrases, and share child-friendly definitions using words the children understand

3rd READ — CHILD TELLS STORY

The third time you read, encourage children to tell you about the key events and how they relate to the characters' thoughts and feelings. As you read, ask questions like "What's happening here?"

The third time you read, encourage children to tell you about the key events and how they relate to the characters' thoughts and feelings. As you read, promote new vocabulary words and ask questions like "What's happening here?"

For this read, before you start, say, "Now that you know this story so well, help me read it. Remember how Sassy felt when she set off on her trip through the jungle? What was she worried about? Let's read and find out." Instead of reading every word, encourage your child to tell you what is happening on each page and how the characters feel about what is happening. Use vocabulary from the book and previous reads to restate what your child says (for instance, if your child says, "She doesn't know how to fit in!" say "Yes, Sassy was worried about making new friends!")

READ Guide: Sassy the Squirrel Monkey

R Repeat the Read

Why do we READ?

When we repeat books with children, we give them the opportunity to hear vocabulary words several times. As we encourage children to become the storytellers and talk about the book, we give them the chance to use language and vocabulary, and they learn empathy as they relate to the characters. By reading this book at least three times, you help children build language and vocabulary, engage in meaningful conversation, and nurture critical thinking. They become powerful, determined learners and problem-solvers.

Read 3 times: transform story time into the ultimate learning experience

1st read: Focus on events: what's happening in the story
2nd read: Focus on emotions: how characters feel
3rd read: The child tells the story: ask "why" question

E Engage & Enjoy

When we keep our children engaged in the book, they are more likely to learn the vocabulary we are teaching and to participate in conversations about the book. Use silly voices, with movement to help keep them focused on the book. Make the most of every opportunity to build vocabulary and model how skilled readers engage with what they read.

Enjoy acting out and explaining **vocabulary** from *Sassy the Squirrel Monkey* to your child. Change your voice to show emotion. Use gestures, actions and sounds, and have the children join you. Point to words and share child-friendly definitions.

Squirrel Monkey:	(point) A small kind of monkey	**Shadow:**	A dark spot made by light shining on something (*show a shadow*)
Compass:	(point) You look at it to find your directions		
Reckless:	Not careful	**"grossly groomed":**	He was messy, not neat
Scurry:	A group of squirrels		
Troop:	A group of one kind of animal	**"scarcely sufficient":**	Not quite enough
Stress:	To worry		

Describe How Sassy feels she doesn't quite fit in

Explain that everyone feels 'different' sometimes, and that Sassy has more ways in which she is alike than different

Ask "What does it feel like to be different from everyone else?"

Talk about different ways you can make someone feel accepted and welcome

A Ask Questions

Conversation about the book is critical. Encourage thinking and talking by asking open-ended questions that begin with "how" or "why" to encourage children to look back in a story and discuss key events and characters' thoughts and feelings related to those events. Children who cannot yet talk can still listen - answer your own questions. Use think-alouds to help children understand important parts of the story. You can say things like, "I wonder why..." or "She must feel..." or even, "Why was Sassy so scared?" (There are no wrong answers.)

D Do More

Make the book come alive. Tie the book to other parts of the day, and connect children to the events of the book.

Look at different animals in classroom or bedroom collections - talk about what makes them "different" and what makes them "the same"

Ask students to share experiences when they may have felt scared. What helped you become brave? What are some things that help your heart "light up"?

Plan a squirrel hunt outside. Create your own compass out of a paper plate and pretend to be a squirrel exploring. Hunt for acorns, count them and sort them by size.

Sassy was ready for her camping celebration.
This squirrel monkey party would be a huge sensation.

As Sassy's mom dropped her off, she gave her advice.
"Make safe and wise choices. Remember to be nice.

"Be careful in the woods. Don't go in there alone.
Here's something to help if you're in a danger zone."

"This is a special compass, Sassy," she heard her mother say,
"if you ever wander or get lost, it helps to guide the way.

"You can wear it as a bracelet, or perhaps like a necklace.
You can clip it on to something; however, don't be reckless.

"Get going, have fun, smile, and make some new friends.
I'll be back later to get you when this ends."

Sassy walked into the party and looked all around,
but just squirrels and just monkeys were only what she found.

Should I squeak with the squirrels or mimic the monkeys?
Sassy thought too long and then felt rather funky.

She walked over to the squirrels and tried to join their scurry, but they were way too busy and all they did was worry.

Sassy worked overtime to blend in and to change,
but the harder she tried, she stood out and looked strange.

She got upset and thought, *This was supposed to be fun,
but it clearly isn't; deeper in the woods I'll run.*

Sassy crept around the back and snuck out from behind.
She quickly got away, with her compass as it shined.

The deeper in the woods she got, her light shined less.
Sassy didn't know which way to turn and then began to stress.

Within the dark shadows, an odd spider monkey loomed.
His light was barely burning and he was grossly groomed.

"I had the same issue with monkeys and with spiders," Spencer growled grimly as he shrugged and sat beside her.

"I tried to be this or that, but never did I fit.
I chose to stay here; it was easier to quit.

"Out here I have enough light, at least just for me.
It's scarcely sufficient, but I can somewhat see."

Spencer turned, then sulked, and headed back to his cave.
He did not say "good-bye," nor did he even wave.

Sassy frowned and saw her light begin to flicker.
She hopped off swiftly to where the woods grew thicker.

As she jumped along trees, her compass fell below, but Sassy kept going because she did not know.

Sassy lost her grip on a branch and tumbled to the ground.
She reached out for her compass, but nowhere could it be found.

Sassy realized she was lost, and she was terrified.
She sat alone in the dark and sobbingly she cried.

"If there's anyone out there, please help me!" Sassy yelled,
with the bit of hope remaining in her heart she held.

Just then, the wind blew, and the moon lit through the trees.
An owl monkey swooped onto a branch in the breeze.

"My name is Sophie. Who are you and how can I help?
What troubles you, dear? Tell me why did you yelp?"

"I'm Sassy, I'm lost, and my compass is gone.
I'm scared and I'm tired," she sighed with a yawn.

"I ran away from the fest 'cause I don't know who to be.
I can't be at the same time both a squirrel and a monkey."

"For your compass to light up, you must be full of love,
and embrace your gifts and talents given from above.

"When you discover yourself and look beneath the surface,
you will find your unique calling and your whole life's purpose.

"What marvels and excites you? What makes you tock and tick? When you're caught up in the moment is when things will click."

Sassy thought about the things she loved for a little while.
Then suddenly, a spark took off and she began to smile.

She felt her heart get strangely warm and noticed in the distance, her compass magically appeared. It lit up and it glistened.

Sassy rushed to her compass, and she held it to her heart.
She realized the light within her had been there from the start.

About the Author

Anna Taylor Stevens is an early childhood educator and mom of an early reader. Through her desire to grow professionally, she discovered Cox Campus and utilized their abundant resources to enhance her teaching skills with her students and with her son, Jack. Anna loves the mountains and snowboarding, which inspired her second book, "Sassy and the 4 C's" (2022 release). The messages in her books are life lessons she wants to share with all children and are also ones adults should remember. Anna lives in south Louisiana with Jack and they love playing basketball in their driveway with friends.

Visit Anna online at SquirrelMonkeyPublishing.com

About the Illustrator

Martina Terzi was born in Livorno, Italy. She spent her childhood falling off her bike and drawing incessantly. Her grandma encouraged her to embrace her artistic gifts and gave her plenty of crayons (and bandages)! After Martina discovered her passion for comic books, she studied to become an illustrator at "Accademia delle Arti Figurative" (Accademy of Figurative Arts) in Florence, Italy. She continued to enhance her skills with fine arts and digital techniques in the UK and Finland. Martina currently lives in Viborg, Denmak, where she drinks a lot of coffee and freelances.

Visit Martina online at martinaterzi.carbonmade.com

CPSIA information can be obtained
at www.ICGtesting.com
Printed in the USA
BVHW021240071121
620782BV00020B/345